The Ethiopian Culture of Ancient Egypt
Hairstyle, Fashion, Food, Recipes and Funerals

Legesse Allyn

AncientGebts.org Press
http://www.ancientgebts.org
http://books.ancientgebts.org

AncientGebts.org Press
http://books.ancientgebts.org

ISBN-13: 978-1519732071
ISBN-10: 1519732074
Library of Congress Control Number: 2016930068

First AncientGebts.org trade paperback edition December 2015

Amarigna and Tigrigna word matching by Legesse Allyn
© Copyright 2015 Legesse Allyn

Scans from the Dover Publications editions of
"The Rosetta Stone" and "An Egyptian Hieroglyphic Dictionary,"
by E.A. Wallis Budge, reprinted by permission of Dover Publications, NY

The Dover Publications editions of "The Rosetta Stone" and
"An Egyptian Hieroglyphic Dictionary" by E. A. Wallis Budge
are available in bookstores and online at http://store.doverpublications.com

Etymologies from Online Etymology Dictioinary reprinted by permission
of Douglas Harper. For more information, etymology footnotes, and
other details, please visit http://www.etymonline.com

Special thanks to:
Aradom Tassew in Addis Ababa, Ethiopia
Ramya Karlapudi in New Delhi, India
Memhr.org Online Tigrigna Dictionary, located at http://memhr.org/dic
AmharicDictionary.com from SelamSoft, Inc., located at http://www.amharicdictionary.com

Doro Wot and Gomen recipes from "Ethiopian Recipes" by reprinted by permission of Daniel Mesfin.

Photo of Diodorus Siculus: Fonte from Wikimedia, Biblioteca di Agira

Cover image: Colorized image by Legesse Allyn

Table of Contents

Introduction

Diodorus Siculus wrote that the culture of ancient Egypt was Ethiopian, due to Ethiopians having founded ancient Egypt and preserving their culture there.

As such, this book provides, through the Ethiopian *Amarigna* and *Tigrigna* languages, a way of learning about the culture of *ancient Egyptian hairstyle, fashion, food, recipes and funerals.*

Ancient texts are messages from the bygone eras. They stand as a testimony to heights of development achieved by our ancient civilizations. Historians for long have depended on ancient texts for understanding contemporary events of ancient periods. These ancient texts give us a first-hand account of the forgotten events, times and culture of the past.

The Rosetta Stone is a singularly important artifact and document that has changed the course of our understanding of Egyptian civilization. The Rosetta Stone enabled historians to bring a purportedly dead language back to life, paving the way for a better understanding of the available hieroglyphic literature. In fact, the language was never dead, thriving in over 30 million speakers.

Although known to ancient Greek historians, like Diodorus Siculus, but unbeknownst to the yesteryear colonial-era historians, the Ethiopian languages of Amarigna and Tigrigna still today hold the elements of the ancient hieroglyphic language intact. These path-breaking revelations are leading to a revision of hitherto translated documents and are giving deeper insights into the Egyptian civilization.

This book provides an understanding of the history and culture of Egyptian civilization by peering through the prism of dual hieroglyphic languages of Amarigna and Tigrigna and analyzing the hieroglyphs, more so, with the help of those of the Rosetta Stone. This approach affords us advantages of not only getting a deeper understanding of historical documents but also an understanding of vast information lying embedded in each of the hieroglyphs.

Meshing hieroglyphs in-between the history of Ancient Egypt, we take a look at their customs, trade and symbology. Another outcome of this exercise is understanding the global relationship between words. It is an accepted fact that more than 60% of the English words have their roots in Latin and Greek, and this book shows Amarigna and Tigrigna to be the root of Greek and Latin and therefore a wide range of European languages including English, Spanish, German and more.

It is demonstrated in this book that many words of the world's languages have their roots in the dual hieroglyphic languages of Amarigna and Tigrigna. Though the extent of such relationships is beyond the scope of this book, it lays foundations for the students to explore this path on their own.

With the world shrinking closer day-by-day and multi-cultural societies a norm, this book paves way for appreciation of the cradle of all the civilizations and how other cultures have readily embraced the elements of ancient Egyptian and therefore Ethiopian culture and civilization. Ancient Egyptian and Ethiopian culture civilized European culture, not the other way around.

This book is also intended to showcase the Ethiopian culture from where the ancient Egyptian culture was born and give the Ethiopian culture its due credit.

ETHIOPIAN HAIR
IN ANCIENT EGYPT
LOVE BRAIDS!

Ethiopian Hair Braiding is Twisting

As you learned in the fist book of this series, according to Diodorus Siculus Ethiopians founded ancient Egypt and continued their traditions in ancient Egypt. This is true of Ethiopian hairstyles.

When we speak of Ethiopia throughout this book series, we are also speaking of Eritrea, which was a part of Ethiopia until 1991, when they became an independent nation.

In Ethiopia, twisting the hair is called asheme, the word seen in the hieroglyph below.

asheme
(a-SHE-me)
"twist hair"

In Ethiopia, braid styles can be very intricate, involving multiple braid styles in one total design. Some braid styles can take up to 12 hours or more.

Photo Credit: Natnael Tadele

4

Ancient Egyptian Braids

African hair is by nature dry and brittle. Even more so in a desert like Egypt. Keeping the hair in a maintainable quality is extremely difficult. It is not merely about washing and conditioning. Below is an ancient Egyptian princess with braids.

The braid style seen on this bust of an ancient Egyptian princess may have taken up to 16 hours or more to complete!

Photo Credit: Guillaume Blanchard

African Hair Can Grow In Very Tiny Curls

Look at the picture below. African hair, such as Ethiopian hair, is formed in a wide range of curl sizes. Some curls as tiny as 1/4", 1/8" or less in diameter.

Photo Credit: Jon Bodsworth

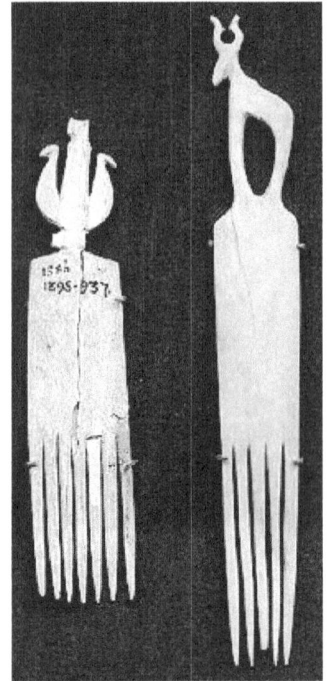

Above we see some ancient Egyptian afro picks. Compare them to the afro pick of today below.

Look at all the tiny little curls!   1/8 inch →| |←

Quick Quiz:
What other cultures are you aware of where women braid their hair?

Braiding Provides a Way to Manage Tiny Curls

Braiding the hair is a natural way for Africans to manage the hair and twist it together in often very artistic styles.

And in Ethiopia, unlike Egypt, it rains for three months out of the year, making braided hair great for rainy conditions, because the braids dry easy and the tiny curls do not have to be combed after getting wet. Plus, braids can stay in the hair for up to 3 months or more before needing to be rebraided.

The braid styles below are simple enough to rebraid nearly every day, probably taking no more than 15 to 30 minutes to complete.

Photo Credit: Rod Waddington

In this way, braiding is not just for style, it provides a very practical purpose for Africans in the caring for their hair.

Cultural Significance

Hairstyles are an integral part of culture. Often braids and dreadlocks are associated with holiness, marital status and other forms of social symbols. Hence, it is essential to understand the role of hairstyles while learning about ancient civilizations.

Quick Quiz:
Why do Ethiopians braid their hair?
Why should one learn about hairstyles while learning history?
Find a hairstyle of another culture and explain about its significance.

How Is African Hair Braided?

Anybody can have his or her hair braided, whether your hair is curly or straight, long or short.

And although the basic steps are the same as for straight hair, the tiny little curls of African hair first have to be combed, stretched and pulled straight. Stretching the tiny curls into long stands of hair is essential for the actual braiding. Then, the hair of the section to be braided is separated into three groupings of hair.

Once all that is done, here is the simplified step-by-step to hair braiding technique. Below we can see the three groupings of hair that will be braided after the curly hair has been stretched.

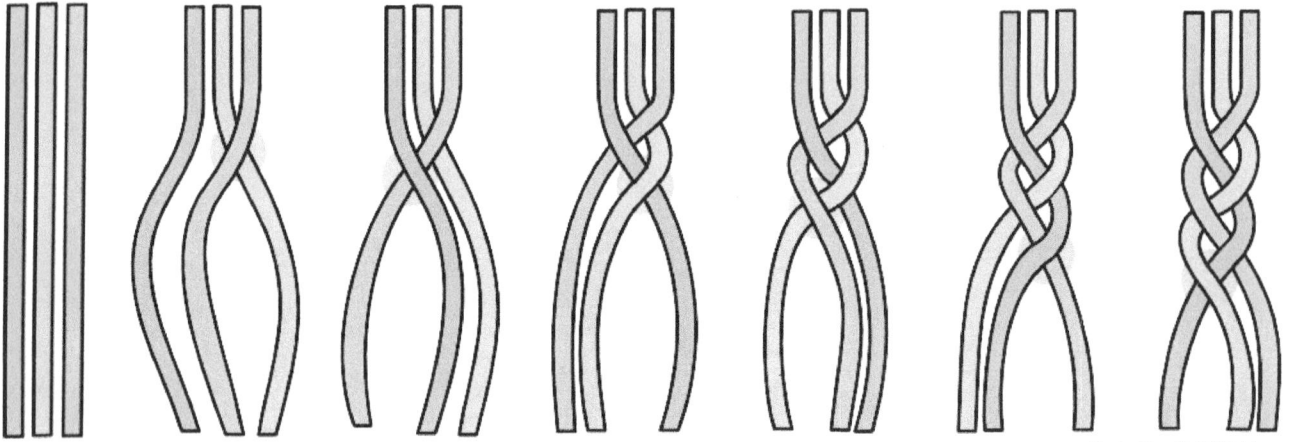

Photo Credit: Stilfehler

Braiding Temporarily Stretches the Hair Into A Style

One way of temporarily stretching the hair is by leaving the hair braided and then the next day unbraiding it. We can see this Ethiopian hair styling technique in the image below.

Photo Credit:Unknown

But when this style gets wet, it reverts back to the tiny curls, so women try not to get their hair wet. While braided, Afican women can go swimming, to the beach, take a shower, or be out in the rain without worrying.

Who would sit through an entire day having their hair braided if it were not a tremendous benefit to the care of their hair? It just shows how important braiding was as part of the ancient Egyptian culture.

Quick Quiz:
How are the tiny curls straightened for braiding?
What sort of importance do you think Egyptians attached to their hairstyle?

Ancient Egyptian Braid Styles for Women

Photo Credit: Unknown

Photo Credit:

Ancient Egyptian Braid Styles for Men

Yes, even African men wear braids, and that included ancient Egyptian men of all professions.

Photo Credit: Estere13

Photo Credit: The Open University

Photo Credit: n·e·r·g·a·l

Even workmen wore braids, as an easier way to manage the hair. These almost look like dreadlocks, which do not exactly involve twisting together strands of hair. They are formed by rubbing the locks of curly hair together. Eventually, as the hair grows and the rubbing continues, the locks grow longer.

Ancient Egyptian Paintings Often Show Braids

Photo Credit: the-tedswoodworking

Look at the picture above. What appears to be an afro in a low-detail painting is often really braided hair, which you can see in the high-detailed painting below. As you saw on the previous page, in some cases, the painting reveals dreadlocks.

Photo Credit: The Yorck Project

And although it can take hours to have one's hair braided, getting up in the morning to go to work and go about one's day is a lot faster, since braids can literally last for months without needing to be rebraided. Today, just a quick spray of oil, gently rubbed into the braids, and it's off to work!

At the end of the day, the workmen could clean their braids or dreadlocks braids so easily, without taking them out. They would simply wet the braids or locks, rub in shampoo and rinse the dirt out!

Shaven Heads Were Popular for Males and Females

Not only were shaven heads popular in ancient Egypt, but still are across Africa today. It is another way of managing the tiny curls, by shaving them off, creating another famous style. Shaven heads are today popular all around the world.

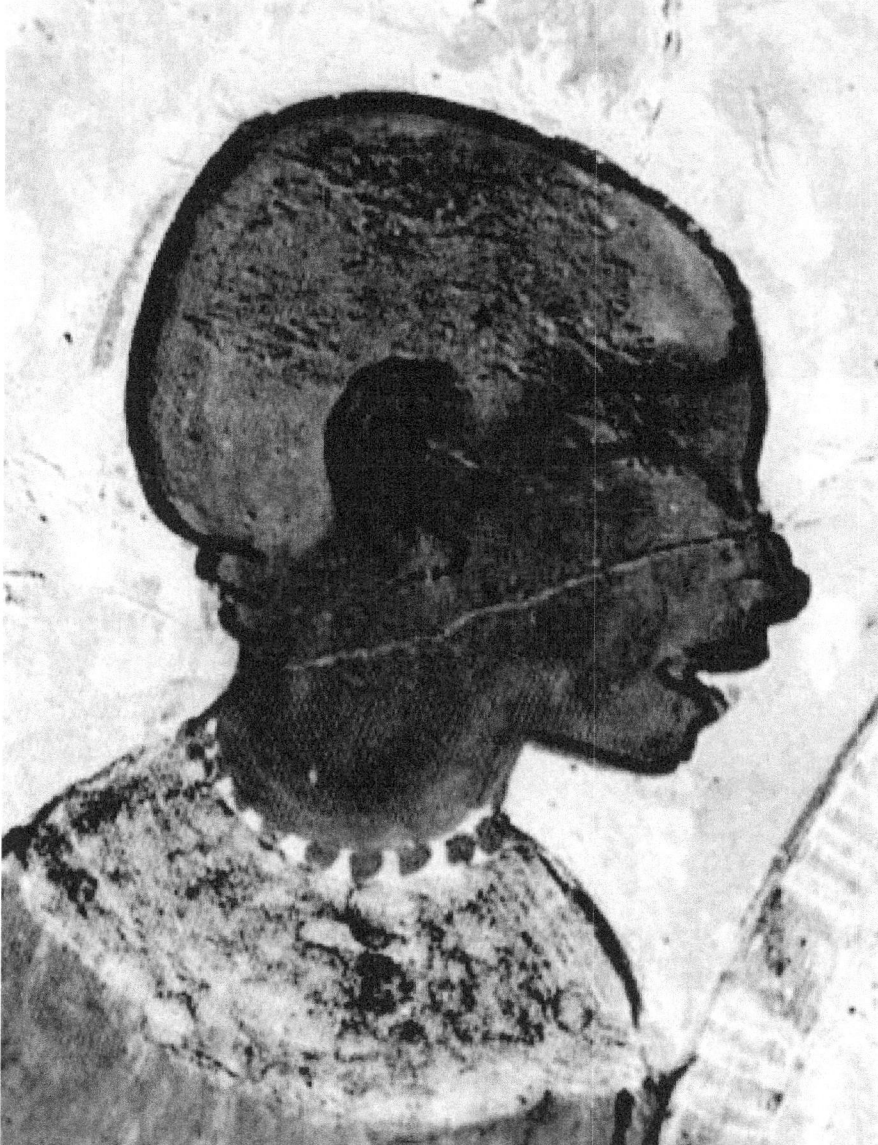

Let's look at the word in hieroglyphs for shaving hair from the head.

Photo Credit: Walters Art Museum

hakhekhe
(ha-KHE-khe)
"erase, delete, scrape"

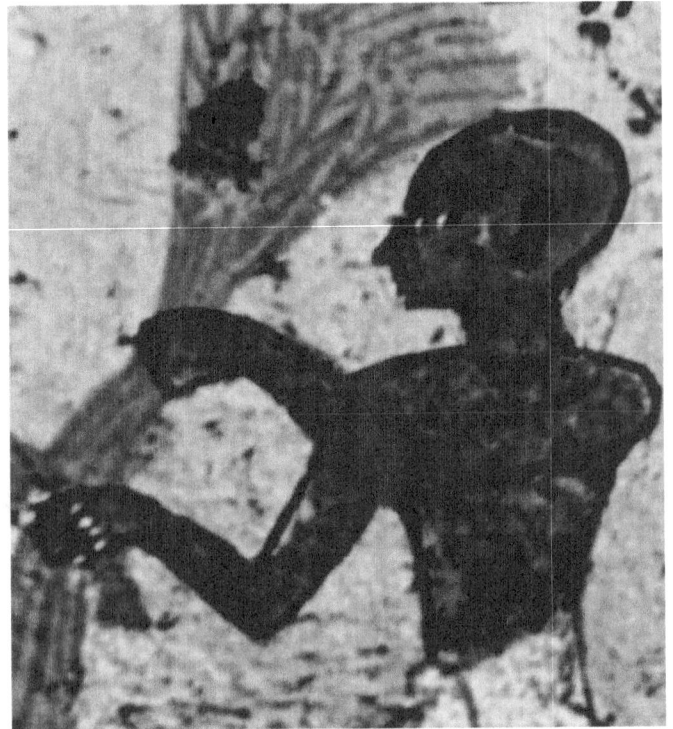

Photo Credit: The Yorck Project

Photo Credit: The Yorck Project

Even Females Wore Shaved Hairstyles

As is still common today across Africa, women wore shaved hairstyles in ancient Egypt. And often in Ancient Egypt, women wore shaven heads under braided hair wigs. Below we see the shaven head of an ancient Egyptian princess.

Photo Credit: Magnus Manske

Photo Credit: Keith Schengili-Roberts

Photo Credit: The Yorck Project

ETHIOPIAN FASHION IN ANCIENT EGYPT

Ethiopian Shema Fabric in Ancient Egypt

Ethiopian fabric is based upon cotton grown in the highlands of Ethiopia and the style continued in ancient Egypt, especially by the royals and upper societies. The Ethiopian word for this style of fabric is *shema* and its production is said to be Ethiopia's oldest industry. Below we see *shema* written in hieroglyphs.

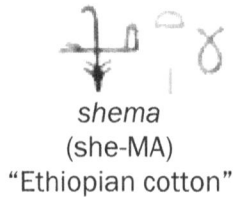

shema
(she-MA)
"Ethiopian cotton"

Shema is still very popular in Ethiopia and is worn by almost everybody. It is often worn in the form of full body wraps, dresses, shawls or sashes. Below you can see how Ethiopian shema looks today.

Photo Credit: Schipul

Quick Quiz:
What is the name given to the traditional fabric of Ethiopia?
Can you recognize the quality of a fabric by its texture?

Thin Ethiopian Cotton Fabric Seen In Paintings

In one royal scene after another, nothing is more apparent than this Ethiopian style of dressing in layers of thin cotton or flax.

Photo Credit: Gardner's Art Through the Ages

Photo Credit: Christopher Saunders

Ethiopian Fabric Is Worn in Fine Thin Layers

Wearing layers of lightly woven cotton has the effect of trapping air between the layers, insulating the wearer from warm or cold temperatures.

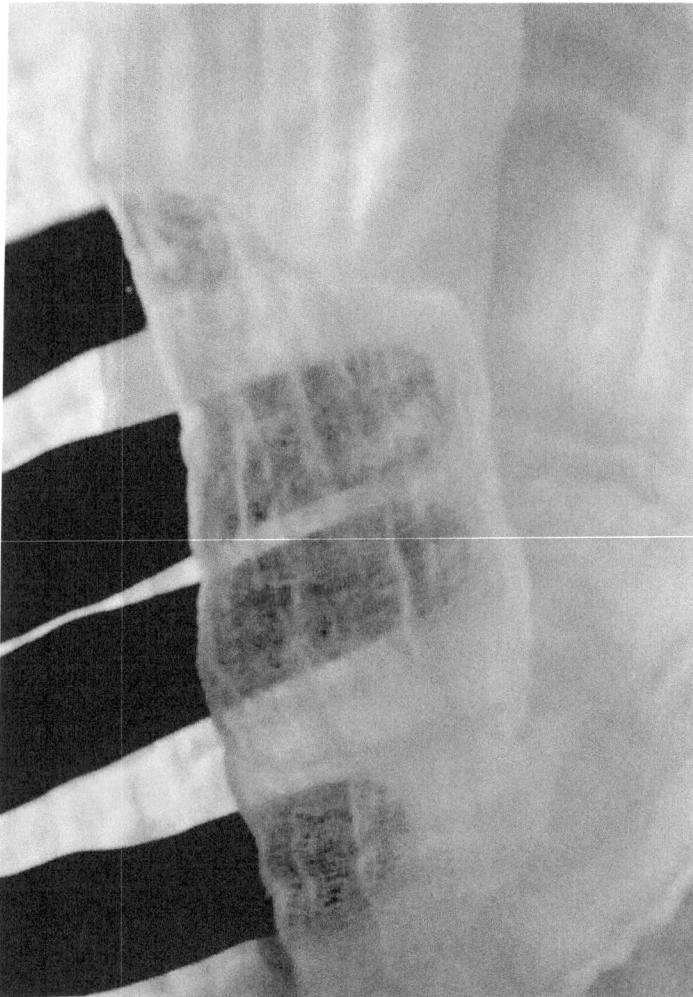

You can see right through. The hieroglyphic word for the fabric reflects both the thinness and the beautiful quality.

ss	tsbuq
(ss)	(ts-BUQ)
"thin, delicate"	"nice, pretty"

Photo Credit: The Yorck Project

Quick Quiz:
Find out what thin fabrics are called as in present day Ethiopia.

Netela, Gabi and Kuta Fabric in Ancient Egypt

Netela or *netsela* is used today by many Ethiopian women to cover their head and shoulders.

Photo Credit: Damien Halleux Radermecker

The name of the fabric depends on the numbers of layers. *Shema* is a single layer, while *netela* is made up of two layers of shema and *gabi* is made out of four layers of shema. *Kuta* is the male version.

Below we see *kuta* written in hieroglyphs.

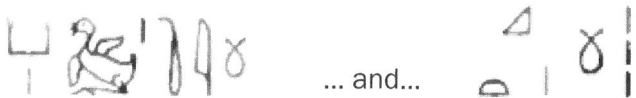

  ... and...

kuta
(ku-TA)
"two-layered fabric worn by men"

Quiz Quiz:
How many layers does *shema* have?
How manby layers does *gabi* have?

More About Clothing

There are other words related to clothing in hieroglyphs. Today, a common word for clothing in Ethiopia is *kdan*, from a word that means to "cover." We see it in hieroglyphs below.

kdan
(ki-DAN)
"uniform, dress, clothes, suit, garment, cover, item of clothing"

Below is the hieroglyph for style of dressing for men. The word *zenete*, means "side of the body."

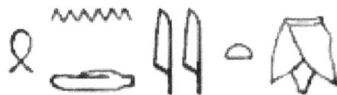

shnt
(shint)
"side of the body"

For women, there is the long dress called a *qelese*. It is put on the body with a series of folds or bends. To the right is an illustration of how this was done, as well as the hieroglyph below.

qelese
(qe-LE-se)
"bend something over"

Quick Quiz:
What is the Egyptian word for something that "covers"?
What is the Egyptian word for a man's skirt?
Name a few queens of ancient Egypt whom you have seen in a *qelese*.

How Was Shema Made In Ancient Egypt?

The handpicked cotton or flax for shema was hand-spun and woven on looms, as you can see in the wooden model from the tomb of Meketre. On the side you can see the hieroglyph for "weave," *shemene.*

Photo Credit: Soutekh67

shemene
(she-ME-ne)
"weave"

If you have not noticed yet, *asheme* (hair braiding), *shemene* (weaving), and *shema* (fabric) are three forms of the same word.

The *shemene* hieroglyph is the spelling out of the word, *shemene,* "weave." Can you see how? Look closely and you see the [S] of *shemene* behind the loom.

If you want to dress like ancient Egyptians, visit your local Ethiopian market and buy shema fabric. Then you can either simply fold it around yourself like a *qelese* or have it sewn into your favorite clothing style. You can also decide how many layers you want.

Having looms and the existence of textiles is an evidence of a job-based economy. How do you think the workers were paid? What was the relation between the loom operator and the workers. These are the kind of questions that you need to ask while learning about ancient civilizations.

Quick Quiz:
What does the word *shemene* mean?
Find out about other ancient cultures that had a loom.
How do means of employment help us understand an ancient society?

Getting Dressed in Ancient Egypt

So now we understand that the Ethiopian rulers of ancient Egypt continued their use of *shema* in ancient Egypt. They also continued using Ethiopian words to describe clothes and getting dressed, as we see below.

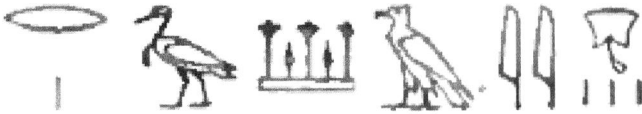

lbs
(lbs)
"clothes, apparel, garment"

Above shows the noun, the name, for clothing in hieroglyphs, while below shows the verb, the action, of getting dressed.

lebese
(le-be-SE)
"get dressed, wear, cover"

In this royal scene, we see two girls helping a woman get dressed. One girl is putting a collar around the woman's neck, while the other girl hands them to her.

Photo Credit: The Yorck Project

Clothing Accessories In Hieroglyphs

Let's look at some words in hieroglyphs that are related to clothing, including some from the Rosetta Stone. One of the most ornate fashion accessories in ancient Egypt was the collar.

kwalaeta
(kwa-LAE-ta)   ... also...
"neck, collar"

chele
(che-LE)
"necklace made of shells and beads"

In a close-up of the painted scene from the previous page, a girl puts a collar around a woman's neck.

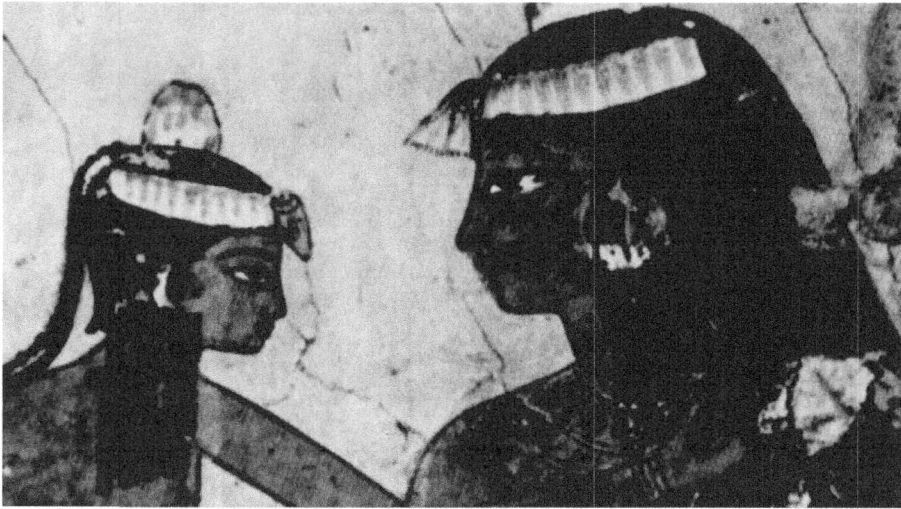

Photo Credit: The Yorck Project

As you may have noticed by now, both *kwalaeta* and *chele* are the same word as the English, *collar*. The English word being recently more derived from the Proto-Indo-European word, *kwol-o*, "neck."

Let's look at some other words in other languages that are the same as *kwalaeta, chele* and *collar*.

collar (n.)

collar	"neck armor, gorget"	(English)
coler	"neck, collar"	(Old French)
cuello	"neck, collar"	(Spanish)
hals	"neck"	(Old Norse and Middle Dutch)
collare	"necklace, band or chain for the neck"	(Latin)
collum	"the neck"	(Latin)
kwol-o	"neck"	(Proto-Indo-European)

Notice that the [C] of *collar*, the [H] of *hals* and the [K] of *kwol-o* are all the same pronunciation through sound change.

Quick Quiz:
What is the relation between *collar, chele* and *kwalaeta*?

25

The Ancient Egyptian Collar

Ancient Egyptian collar pieces were elaborate pieces of art, combining beads and gold attached by wire. We can see an example below.

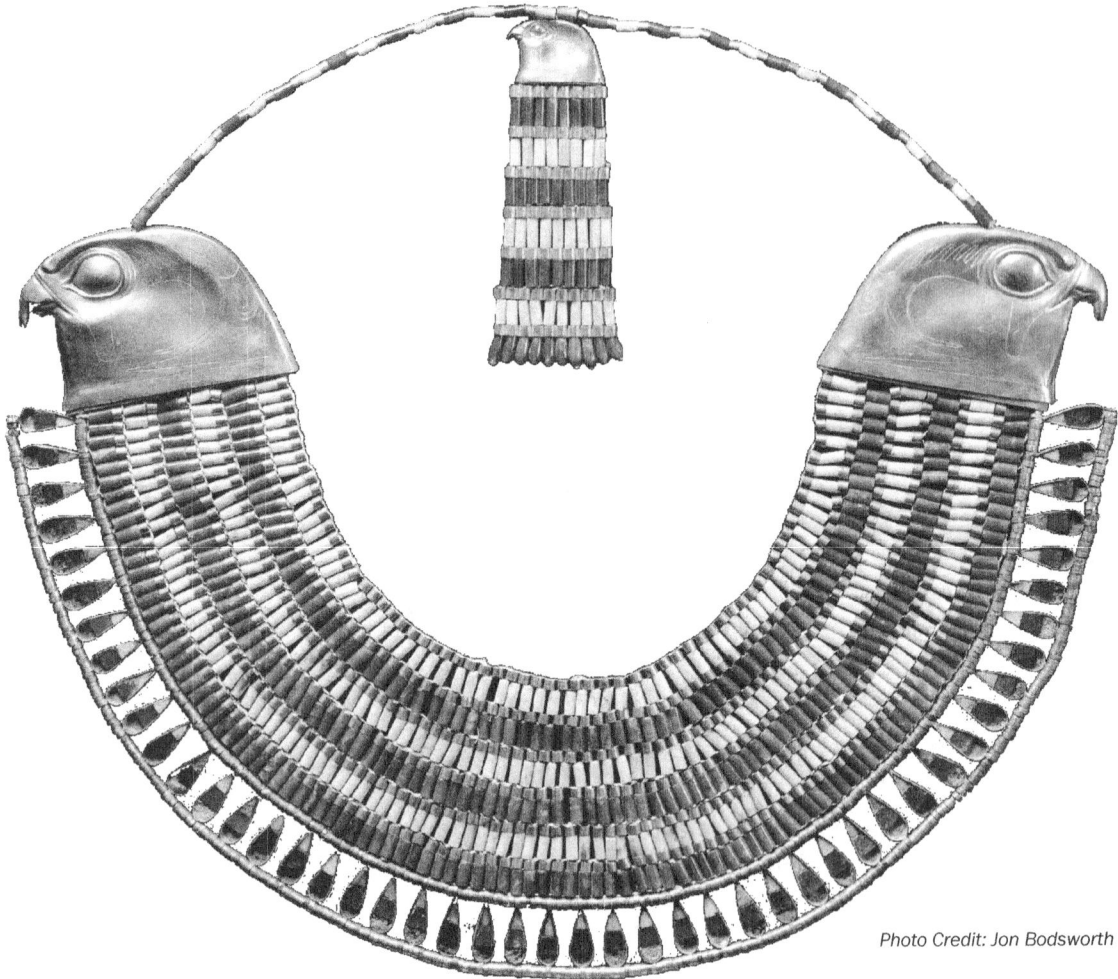

Photo Credit: Jon Bodsworth

In two hieroglyphs for "wire, cord" we can clearly see the wire in the illustration following the hieroglyphic spelling out of the word, *shbo*.

shbo
(shi-BO)
"wire, cord"

Quick Quiz:
Based on the ornate gold falcon heads at each end of the collar, who might it have belonged to?
What else can you understand on seeing a necklace?
What is the Egyptian word for wire or cord?

Ancient Egyptian Rings

Another fashion accessory ancient Egyptians wore were rings, as seen below.

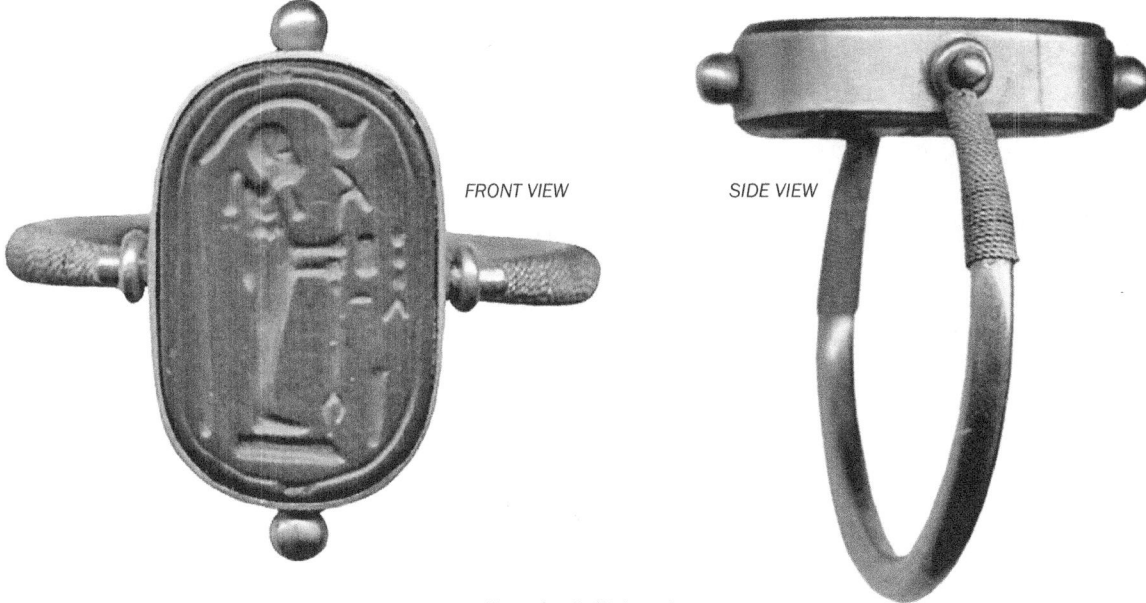

FRONT VIEW   *SIDE VIEW*

Photo Credit: Walters Art Museum

Let's look at the "ring" hieroglyph, with an illustration of a ring following the hieroglyphic spelling.

katim
(ka-TIM)
"ring"
("ring" in the Rossetta Stone)

And what did the ring go onto? The finger, of course.

tat
(tat)
"finger"

Quick Quiz:
Do you know what does the word "metallurgy" mean?
What does the ability of the civilization to produce rings reveal to you?

Other Fashion Accessories in Ancient Egypt

Below we see the hieroglyph for the word, "belt," *qebeto*, another clothing accessory.

Photo Credit: Guillaume Blanchard

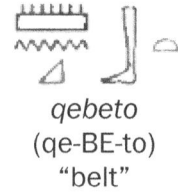

qebeto
(qe-BE-to)
"belt"

Photo Credit: Natnael Tadele

Quick Quiz:

What are the fashion accessories commonly used by you and the Egyptians?

How To Put On Clothing and Clothing Accessories

Now we move on from the clothing items and clothing accessories to how to put them on the body. This first word appears in the Rosetta Stone and represents the adorning of the body.

masamer
(ma-SA-mer)
"adorn"
("robe the Gods" in the Rosetta Stone)

And as seen below, *anegete* is a word for both something worn around the neck and the neck itself, as was the case with the previous word, *kwalaeta*.

anegete   *anget*
(a-ne-GE-te)   (an-GET)
"strap on, carry on one's shoulders"   "neck"

Of course, you may have already noticed *anget* is the same word that the English *neck* comes from. Also, the word *anga vastramu* in Telugu (a language spoken in India) is a cloth (*vastramu*) strapped on shoulder or around the neck (*anga*). Like *the English word neck,* the Telugu *anga* also appears to have its roots from *anegete*.

In this next word, we can see how to put on clothing, a necklace, collar, waist decoration or clothing. The item is put on so that it encircles the neck, waist, or body.

akhbebe
(aKHE-be-be)
"surround, encircle"

Again, the spelling is not necessarily spelling the word for the illustration. Here the word is spelling out a verb, the action of putting on what is illustrated. Fascinating, right?

Did you know there were so many terms in hieroglyphs just for things that were put around the neck or body?

Spread, Connect and Wrap

Below is the hieroglyphic word that describes how to put something around the neck or body, *asasa*, "spread out" before connecting it or tying it together.

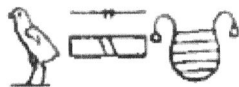

asasa
(a-SA-sa)
"set apart, spread out"

So, here again the hieroglyphic word is a verb, an action, spelled out in hieroglyphic letters that describe something related to the illustration.

Let's look at another hieroglyph that describes a verb, an action, associated with the illustration following the hieroglyphic spelling. We can see from the word spelled out in hieroglyphs that the illustration is that of two objects connected together.

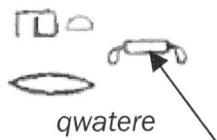

qwatere
(qwa-TE-re)
"tie together, connect, tie up"

Another word that has to do with how to get dressed is the word *temteme*, "wrap, wear," which we can see in hieroglyphs below.

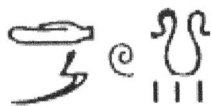

temteme
(te-me-TE-me)
"wrap, wind, wear"

Quick Quiz:
Name a few fashion accessories used by the Egyptians. Trace and then draw a few of the hieroglyphs.
Name a few verbs you have learned so far. Trace and then draw a few of the hieroglyphs.

COOKING & EATING
ANCIENT EGYPTIAN FOOD

Nutritional Diets Were Written and Maintained

While ancient Egyptians could generally eat anything, ancient Egyptian kings were provided with a strict written diet to be followed daily, prescribed by the king's doctor.

"And it was the custom for the kings to partake of delicate food, eating no other meat than veal and duck, and drinking only a prescribed amount of wine, which was not enough to make them unreasonably surfeited or drunken. And, speaking generally, their whole diet was ordered with such continence that it had the appearance of having been drawn up, not by a lawgiver, but by the most skilled of their physicians, with only their health in view."
Diodorus book 1, 70:11-12

Photo Credit: The Yorck Project

Food Was Brought To Ancient Egypt from Ethiopia

With the introduction of food crops and farming to Egypt by Ethiopian farmers and merchants, food became plentiful in ancient Egypt. So plentiful and important was the food, that the Ethiopian merchants were made the kings.

Photo Credit: Lars

"When men, they say, first ceased living like the beasts and gathered into groups, at the outset they kept devouring each other and warring among themselves"
Diodorus book 1, 90:1

Ethiopian Food in Ancient Egypt was Delicious!

Below you see a typical Ethiopian meal.

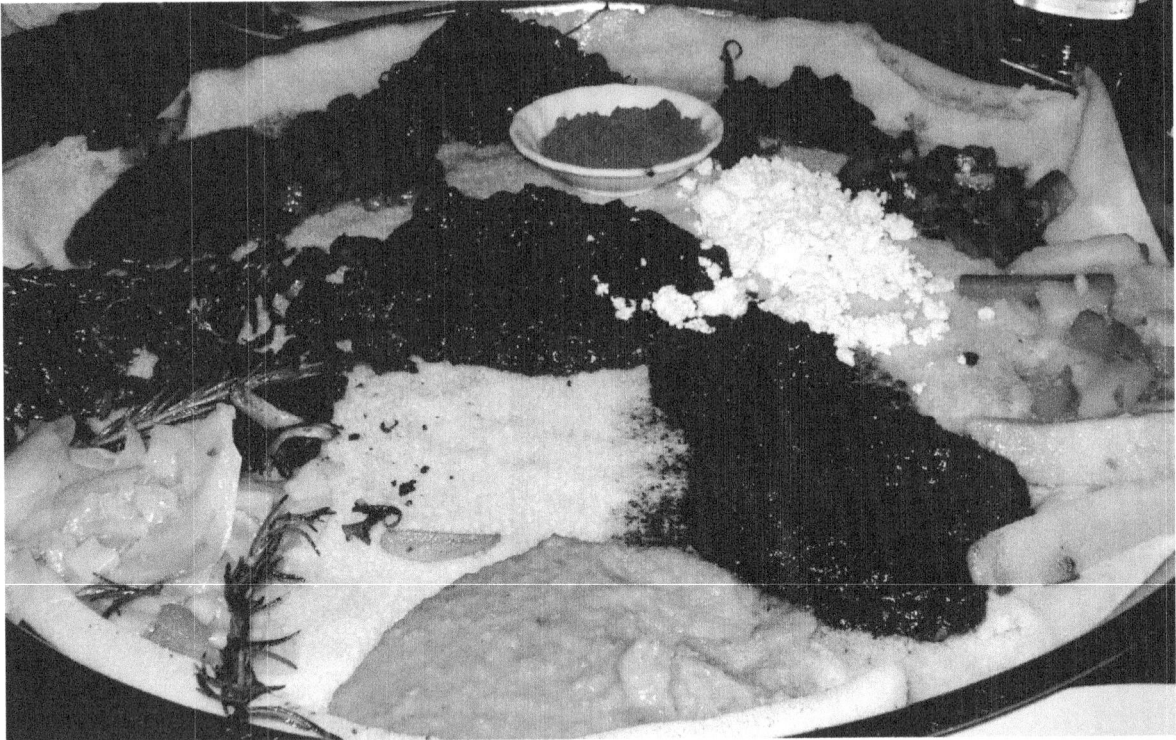

The names of still-popular Ethiopian food dishes are shown below in hieroglyphs. Let's see some of the names in hieroglyphs.

tsebhi
(tseb-HEE)
"sauce, soup, spiced beef/chicken/vegetables/fish stew"

Related to *tsebhi* is the dish loved by Ethiopians, *tibs*, which is roasted meat with onions, spiced butter, and spices.

tibs
(ti-BS)
"roasted meat"

wat
(wat)
"spicy Ethiopian stew"

Quick Quiz:
Briefly describe the dietary patterns of Ancient Egyptians.
Name a few dishes of the ancient Egypt. Trace and then draw the hieroglyphs.

Onions

In ancient Egypt, as in Ethiopia, onions formed the base for cooking meals.

Photo Credit: Liz West

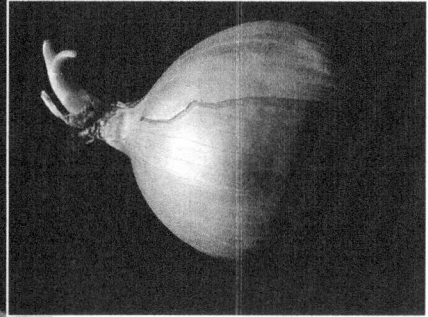

Photo Credit: Dnor

Below you can see the word for "onion" in hieroglyphs. The hieroglyphic spelling of "white" is followed by an illustration of a round onion, as we see below.

hecha
(he-CHA)
"white"

And below we see the word for onions as merchandise.

aq'ha
(aq-HA)
"object, item, thing, merchandise"

Quick Quiz:
Does *hecha* describe the onion's color or is it the word for onion?
Trace and then draw the *white onion* hieroglyph.

LET'S COOK ETHIOPIAN FOOD!

Let's Cook Ethiopian Food from Ancient Egypt!

Doro Wot
(Chicken in Hot Sauce and Boiled Egg)

Photo Credit: AmelGhouila

Ethiopian cuisine is spicy and delicious. A favorite is *Doro Wot* (do-ro wot). *Doro Wot* is made with onions, Ethiopian spices, chicken, and boiled eggs. It is dished onto a plate or platter covered with an injera. The food is eaten by picking some up with a piece of another injera and putting it in your mouth.

INGREDIENTS

    1 medium chicken (cut into pieces with skin removed)
    4 medium red onions
    1/2 to 2 cups nitir qibe butter (Ethiopian spiced butter)
    1 tablespoon to 1/2 cup berbere pepper (Ethiopian hot pepper)
    1/4 teaspoon cardamom   1/4 teaspoon garlic powder
    1/4 teaspoon black pepper   1/2 teaspoon ginger
    1/4 teaspoon bishop's weed   1/2 teaspoons salt
    1/2 cup Tej (Ethiopian honey wine)
    4 cups water
    6 eggs

    Large bowl
    Large pot
    Small pot

In a large pot, fry chopped red onions, without any oil, on low heat until tender and golden brown.

After onions are brown, add the spiced butter, stirring gently until melted. Add the berbere Ethiopian hot pepper and stir gently. Stir in 1/2 cup of the 4 cups of water. Stir in the *tej* honey wine. Add the cardamom, garlic powder, and ginger and stir well. Rinse off the cut up chicken and add to the pot. Cook over medium-low heat for 35-40 minutes.

While that is cooking, boil the 6 eggs in the smaller pot for 15-20 minutes. When they are done, peel off the eggshells and rinse off eggs. Set aside.

Gently stir in the rest of the water. Add the salt and pepper. Simmer over very low heat for 10 minutes more. Add the boiled eggs and stir very gently.

Gomen
(Spiced Collard Greens)

Photo Credit: Chaojoker

INGREDIENTS

1 pound fresh collard greens
1 medium red onion (chopped)
2 cups water
1/2 teaspoon garlic powder
1/2 teaspoon salt (or add more to your taste)
2 cups nitir qibe
1/4 cup vegetable oil

Medium pan

First, wash the collard greens and boil in medium pot until soft. Then remove from the pot and cut up in small pieces after draining water off.

Brown the chopped onions in the medium pan, without oil, until golden brown and tender. Add oil and collard greens and cook for 10 minutes.

Quick Quiz:
List different cuisines that you are aware of from countries other than your own.
What other cuisines have you tasted other than your own country's?

Eating The Meal

Serve the doro wot and collard greens on a plate or platter that is covered with injera.

Photo Credit: YngRich

From a separate injera, tear off a piece the size of your palm and use it to pick up the food, as you see diners doing in the photo above. Eat the injera and the food inside of it together by putting the entire thing in your mouth! So don't pick up too much.

There are a number of delicious Ethiopian drinks available including the delicious sweet Ethiopian honey wine *tej*, used in the Doro Wot recipe, available at the Ethiopian and Eritrean markets.

Prepared injera is also available from Ethiopian and Eritrean markets. For other delicious Ethiopian recipes look for the book by Daniel Mesfin entitled "Exotic Ethiopian Cooking" from Ethiopian Cookbook Enterprises.

Quick Quiz:
Name a few Ethiopian drinks. Trace and then draw a few of the hieroglyphs.

Pick Up Food with Injera and Eat!

Injera is used to eat Ethiopian food and was likely eaten in ancient Egypt, especially because you cannot eat *tsebhi*, *tibs* or almost any other kind of Ethiopian food without it. Injera is commonly made with tef flour, although it can be made with wheat flour, too.

Photo Credit: PhoTom

There has been a lot of research into *tef*. The *tef* in injera is high in dietary fiber and iron, providing protein and calcium to the meal.

According to Denis J. Murphy in his book, *People, Plants, and Genes: The Story of Crops and Humanity*, as well as ancient Greek historian Diodorus Siculus, Ethiopians were among the first to domesticate plants and animals for food, especially in the Ethiopian highlands. And *tef* was one of the earliest plants domesticated there. So it is no surprise that *tef* injera was likely eaten in ancient Egypt by its Ethiopian founders and royalty.

Quick Quiz:
What is *tef*?
What nutirents is *tef* rich in?
Who eats *tef* today?

Injera Is Made With Tef Flour

Injera is generally made of flour from *tef* grain, shown in hieroglyphs below. Tef grains are very tiny and are indicated in the hieroglyph by the illustration of grains that follows the spelling of the word *tef*.

tef
(tef)
"tef grain (used to make injera)"

Photo Credit: Rasbak

Photo Credit: Rasbak

And another reason tef injera was likely used to eat *tsebhi, tibs* and *wat* is because there is a hieroglyph for *tef* as "bread," too, that you can see below.

tef
(tef)
"tef bread"

In fact, by looking at the letters that spell *tef*, you can see the first hieroglyphic letter is that of the popular Ethiopian bread called, *dabo*. If you remember from book one, the [D] and [T] pronunciations are related, so the *tef* [T] pronunciation can be spelled with the *dabo* [D].

Quick Quiz:
Explain the hieroglyph of tef. Trace and the draw the *tef* hieroglyph.
What are some of the different type of grains available for the manufacture of bread in addition to *tef*?

42

Spices Made Ancient Egyptian Food Taste Great!

Spices turn an ordinary meal into an exciting one. And in ancient Egypt there was one particular spice that people cannot live without in Ethiopia, *berbere*. It is a combination of pepper and other spices that make Ethiopian food unique.

Photo Credit: Badagnani

And in ancient Egypt, *tsebi, tibs* and *wat* would have required generous portions of *berbere*. We can see the hieroglyph for *berbere* below.

berbere
(ber-BE-re)
"red chili pepper, spice"

Quick Quiz:
Find out the ingredients of *berbere*.
Trace and then draw the *berbere* hieroglyph.

Poultry and Eggs

Below we can see workers in a poultry farm processing poultry.

Photo Credit: Matthias Seidel, Abdel Ghaffar Shedid: Das Grab des Nacht. Art and history
of an official tomb of the 18th dynasty in Western Thebes, of Saverne, Mainz 1991

We can see the hieroglyphic word below for what is today in Ethiopia the word for a hen or chicken.

doro
(DO-ro)
"chicken, hen"

Some eggs and chicks.

Photo Credit: The Yorck Project

Fats and oils

While *qibe* is a general word for oil, *niter qibe* has a special place in Ethiopian food today and likely in ancient Egypt. This is because *qibe* is essential for cooking *tsebi, tibs* and *wat*.

Photo Credit: Rainer Z

We can see the hieroglyph for *qibe* below.

qibe
(qi-BAY)
"oil, ointment, grease, cream"

Quick Quiz:
What is *niter qibe* made up of?
What is the hieroglyphic word for oil and grease. Trace and then draw the hieroglyph.

Salt

And what is delicious food without a pinch of salt? Did you ever wonder from where salt, called *chaw* in ancient Egypt and Ethiopia still today, comes from? Below salt is being mined in Ethiopia's Danakil Desert.

Photo Credit: Ji-Elle

If you look closely at the tools they are using to cut up the slabs of salt. You might remember the tools from ancient Egyptian art and artifacts.

Below is salt in hieroglyphs.

chaw
(chaw)
"salt"

Photo Credit: Ji-Elle

netsele
(ne-TSE-le)
"detach"

Quick Quiz:
Find out the name of the tool being used to mine the salt? Trace and then draw the *chaw* hieroglyph. Find out the methods in which salt is manufactured today?

Water

Water is essential to life. We would not exist without it. There are two important words for water in ancient Egypt and they are words for water all over the world. Let's look at two words for "water" in hieroglyphs, *may* and *wha*.

Photo Credit: JJ Harrison

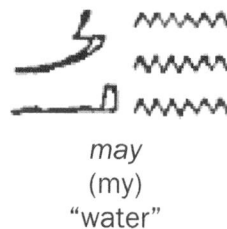

may
(my)
"water"

Photo Credit: Malene Thyssen

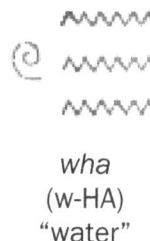

wha
(w-HA)
"water"

The two words are the source for "water" in many languages, including English.

may:			**wha:**		
	amay	"water" (Cherokee)		ha	"water" (Mayan)
	mayim	"water" (Hebrew)		awa	"water" (Maori – Australia/ New Zealand)
	omi	"water" (Yoruba)		hē	"drink" (Chinese)
	amay	"water" (Cherokee)		wei	"water" (Hawaiian)
	mây	"cloud" (Vietnamese)		ahua	"water" (Gothic)
	maya	"water" (Arabic)		⟶ became:	aqua "water" (Latin)
	umi	"ocean" (Japanese)			agua "water" (Spanish)
	ami	"rain" (Japanese)		wa-a-tar	"water" (Proto-Indo-European)
	mul	"water" (Korean)		⟶ became:	water "water" (English)

Quick Quiz:
What is the word for "water" in the language(s) you speak?
Trace and then draw the *may* and *wha* hieroglyphs.

Milk

Ancient Egyptians drank milk and used milk to cook and bake. Below you can see an ancient Egyptian man milking a cow.

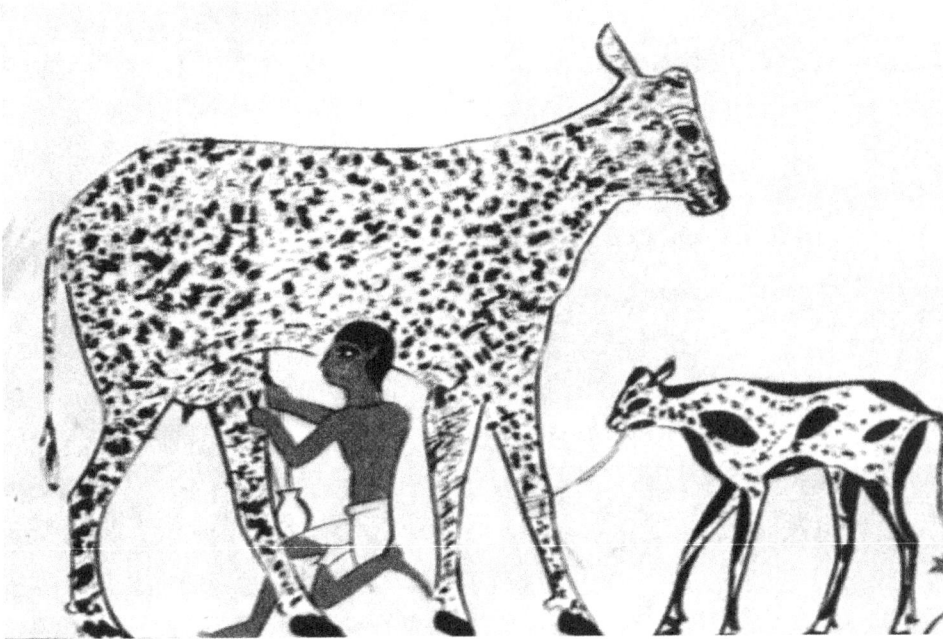

Photo Credit: 1000 Fragen an die Natur

In the hieroglyph below you can see the same milk container that the man above is using. The hieroglyphic word below is to "transport" milk, or transport anything, the hieroglyphic word *mechan*.

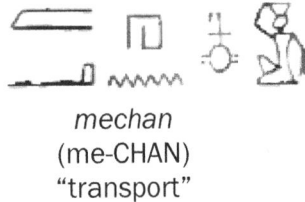

mechan
(me-CHAN)
"transport"

A dairy operation.   *Photo Credit: Keith Schengili-Roberts*

Quick Quiz:
Do you see any similarities between the Egyptian word for transport and present day English words?

Wine

Ancient Egyptians drank wine, which they made from grapes, as well as honey.

Photo Credit: Das Grab des Nacht

Below we see the hieroglyph for harvesting grapes.

weyni areye
(why-NEE a-RE-ye)
"bring in the grape harvest"

Quick Quiz:
What are the various wines associated with different countries?
Trace and then draw the *wine harvest* hieroglyph.

Honey Wine

Honey was also used to brew honey wine, as is still done in Ethiopia today, called *tej*. We can see organic honey below, still in the honeycomb.

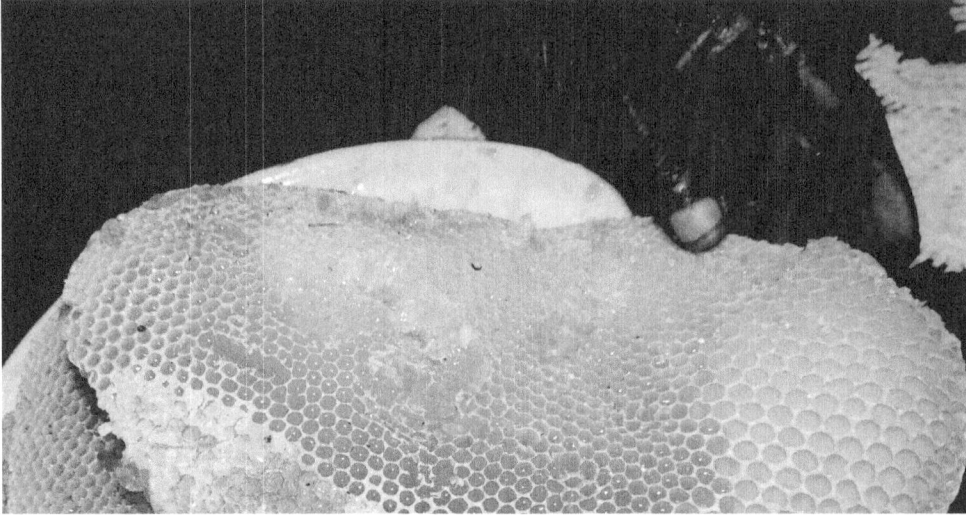

Photo Credit: Elias Mulugeta Hordofa

Tej as it is brewed today in Ethiopia.

Photo Credit: Ji-Elle

Beer

Beer was brewed in ancient Egypt. In Ethiopia today, it is still called *tela* and *swa*. Below are hieroglyphs for both beer.

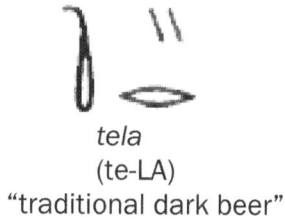

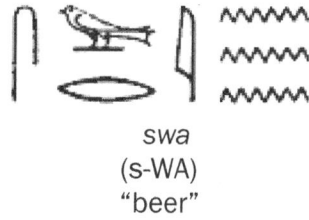

tela
(te-LA)
"traditional dark beer"

swa
(s-WA)
"beer"

Above we see a light-colored Ethiopian beer.

Quick Quiz:
What are the different grains from which beer is made?
Trace and then draw the *tela* and *swa* hieroglyphs.

This wooden model of an ancient Egyptian factory, from the tomb of Meketre, shows a bakery and brewery.

AFTER LIFE IN ANCIENT EGYPT

When Life is Over

Death is a natural part of life. In hieroglyphs, a man with a hatchet indicates death or one's demise.

mot
(mote)
"death, demise"

In ancient Egypt, the beetle represented the burying of the dead. While the "burying beetle" (*sexton beetle*) is known for burying dead rodents and birds to insert its eggs into, the Egyptian scarab beetle (*scaraabaeus beetle*) did something similar. After inserting its eggs into a ball of dung, it rolled it into a hole in the ground, burying the ball. In the course of time its eggs will hatch.

berero
(be-RE-ro)
"cockroach, beetle"

In this way, the scarab beetle and other burying beetles are the undertakers of the insect world. In hieroglyphs, *qebere* means "bury."

qebere
(qe-BE-re)
"bury"

The purpose of burying the body of the deceased was to hide away the body and cover it, as we can see from the hieroglyphs below. In fact, the English word *hell* is from the Proto-Indo-European word for "cover," *kel*, both words derived from the word *kelela* of the ancient Egyptian language, seen on the right below. Thankfully, as you can see in the *kelela* hieroglyph, *hell* is simply a tomb cover and not a pit in the middle of the earth!

shegore
(she-GO-re)
"hide away, lock"

kelela
(ke-LE-la)
"a cover"

Quick Quiz:
What does the beetle represent for Ancient Egyptians? Trace and then draw the *berero* hieroglyph.
What do the hieroglyphs of burials mean? Trace and then draw the *qebere* hieroglyph.

Shrines Commemorated Life

Shrines often are shown with a platform, as is shown in hieroglyphs below.

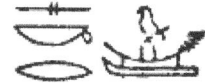

Photo Credit: Jon Bodsworth

statue

base

aqwemete
(a-qwe-ME-te)
"deposit"
(as shown in the Rosetta Stone)

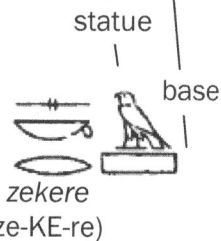

zekere
(ze-KE-re)
"commemorate"
(as shown in the Rosetta Stone)

Quick Quiz:
Why do you think a shrine is represented on a platform?
In real life, do you find any relationship between symbols you give respect to and their height?

There Were Many Ways To Remember Life

Below we see a shrine on a skiff.

Photo Credit: The Egyptian Book of the Dead: The Book of Going Forth by Day by James Wasserman et al.

zekere
(ze-KE-re)
"commemorate"
(as shown in the Rosetta Stone)

Quick Quiz:
What does the hieroglyphic *zekere* mean?
Trace and then draw the *zekere* hieroglyph above.

Boats As Shrines

When you see a boat on a platform, it is likely a shrine. Let's look at the difference below.

Photo Credit: Unknown

This is a shrine on a platform

zekere
(ze-KE-re)
"commemorate"
(as shown in the Rosetta Stone)

merkab
(mer-KAB)
"boat"
(as shown in the Rosetta Stone)

Below is a boat in the water. Notice it is not on a platform and the oar is in the water.

Photo Credit: The Egyptian Book of the Dead: The Book of Going Forth by Day by James Wasserman et al.

Quick Quiz:
In ancient Egyptian art, how can you differentiate between a boat that is part of a shrine and a regular boat?
Trace and then draw the *merkab* hieroglyph.

Small Houses As Shrines

Below is a portable shrine as mentioned in the Rosetta Stone.

qeyae
(qe-YAE)
"living place"
("shrine" in the Rosetta Stone)

Below are other hieroglyphs for other types of shrines.

nius
(ni-OOS)
"small"

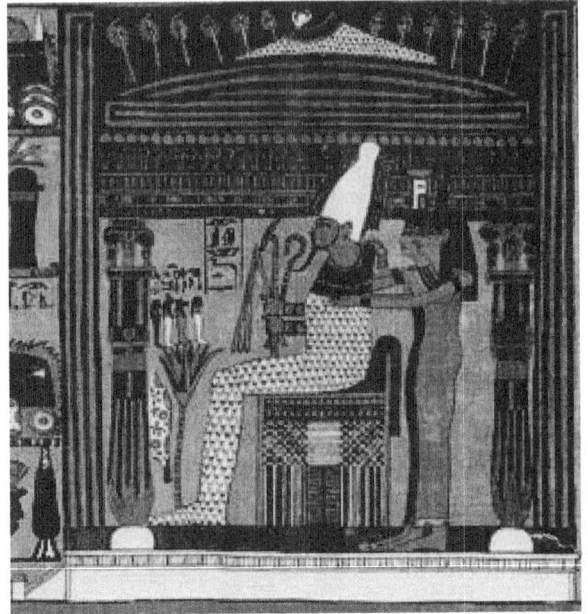
Photo Credit: Soutekh67

Two surviving small shrines.

Photo Credit: HoremWeb

Photo Credit: Olaf Tausch

Quick Quiz:
What are different words used for shrines by the Egyptians?
Trace and then draw the hieroglyphs of the different types of shrines above.

What Is a Shrine?

The hieroglyphs of the word for shrine, *zekere*, as shown in the Rosetta Stone, are seen below,

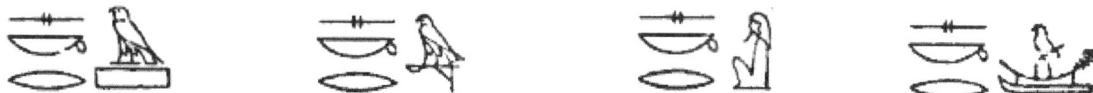

zekere
(ze-KE-re)
"commemorate"

The word *shrine* is derived from the word, *zekere*, "commemorate." Read the etymology below, showing how pronunciation sound change affected *zekere* in different languages. The etymologies in this book series come from the Online Etymology Dictionary, located at www.etymonline.com.

shrine (n.)

scrinium	"case or box for keeping papers"	(Latin)
scrin	"ark (of the covenant); chest, coffer; case for relics"	(Old English)
shrine	"a tomb of a saint (usually elaborate and large)	(English)
schrijn	"shrine"	(Dutch)
schrein	"shrine"	(German)
skrynya	"shrine"	(Russian)
skrine	"shrine"	(Lithuanian)

(see http://www.etymonline.com/index.php?term=shrine)

But to have a fuller understanding of the purpose of the shrine, let's look at *commemorate* and other forms of the word. What is commemoration? Read the definition below.

commemorate (v.)
- to exist or be done in order to remind people of (an important event or person from the past)
- to do something special in order to remember and honor (an important event or person from the past)

   (see http://www.merriam-webster.com/dictionary/commemorate)

> *zkr*   (zi-KIR)   "commemoration"
> This is the honoring of the Ancestor.
>
> *tezekere*   (te-ze-KE-re)   to ask"
> This is making a request of the Ancestor, with the [te-] verb prefix.
>
> *azekere*   (a-ze-KE-re)   "bring attention to"
> This is the shrine as a place for people to visit to remember the Ancestor, with the [a-] verb prefix.

Quick Quiz:
What was the relation between a *shrine* and *zekere*?

What is Relationship of the Words Zekere and Sacred?

Read the etymology for the word *sacred* below.

sacred (adj.)

sacren	"to make holy"	(English)
sagrado	"sacred"	(Spanish)
sacrer	"consecrate, anoint, dedicate"	(Old French)
sacrare	"to make sacred, consecrate; hold sacred; immortalize; set apart, dedicate,"	(Latin)
sacer	"sacred, dedicated, holy, accursed,"	(Old Latin)
sak	"to sanctify."	(Proto-Indo-European)

(see http://www.etymonline.com/index.php?term=sacred)

"Now the Ethiopians, as historians relate, were the first of all men... to honour the gods and to hold sacrifices and processions and festivals and the other rites by which men honour the deity."
Diodorus, book 3, 2:1-2

The Relationship of the Words Zekere and Sacrifice

So what is a *sacrifice*, which you should be able by now to see it is the same word as *zekere*. Let's look at the etymology.

sacrifice (n.)

sacrifice	"offering of something (especially a life) to a deity as an act of propitiation or homage"	(English)
	"that which is offered in sacrifice"	(English)
sacrifise	"sacrifice, offering"	(Old French)
sacrificium	"performing priestly functions or sacrifices,"	(Latin)
sacra	"sacred rites"	(Latin)
sacrificio	"sacrifice"	(Spanish)

(see http://www.etymonline.com/index.php?term=sacrifice)

Therefore, the shrine provides a way of honoring the deceased person, a place to come and remember him or her, as well as a place to come and view the symbol of the deceased person and ask for divine help here on earth.

Quick Quiz:
What is the relationship between *zekere* and *sacred*?

FUNERALS, GIFTS & EULOGIES

Food & Gifts Were Deposited On Altars

Photo Credit: The Egyptian Book of the Dead: The Book of Going Forth by Day by James Wasserman et al.

altars

aqwemete
(a-qwe-ME-te)
"deposit"
(as shown in the Rosetta Stone)

Quick Quiz:
What is the Egyptian word for an altar? Trace and then draw the *aqwemete* hieroglyph.
From what you have learned about ancient Egypt so far, list a few things that Egyptians would have deposited at the altar?

Jars of Contributions Were Weighed & Recorded

In the scene below from the *Papyrus of Ani*, the man on the left has brought a container full of an offering as a contribution to a monument for Ani, who was a Chief Examiner according to the papyrus.

You can see the container on the scale behind the man. The Ibis represents a clerk recording and judging the amount in the container that the man has brought. Is the contribution enough?

Photo Credit: Eternal Egypt: Masterworks of Ancient Art from the British Museum by Edna R. Russmann

Container filled with an offering

habe
(ha-BE)
"grant, deliver, confer, give, supply, provide, bestow"
("bestowed" in the Rosetta Stone)

Quick Quiz:
What does the ibis represent according to the Egyptian legends?
What is the Egyptian word for "bestowed"? Trace and then draw the *habe* hieroglyph.

The Body Was Prepared for the Funeral & Burial

In the scene below, we see the final preparation of a coffin for the body, as women cry in front of the coffin containing the body.

Photo Credit: see www.webcitation.org/63YCN7sEt

"But during this interval they had made splendid preparations for the burial, and on the last day, placing the coffin containing the body before the entrance to the tomb, they set up, as custom prescribed, a tribunal to sit in judgment upon the deeds done by the deceased during his life."
Diodorus book 1, 72:4

The Nation Grieved The Passing of The Deceased

Those who were beloved were grieved by those mourning them.

Photo Credit: The Yorck Project

These women are all crying, too, with tears streaming down their faces.

"For when any king died all the inhabitants of Egypt united in mourning for him, rending their garments, closing the temples, stopping the sacrifices, and celebrating no festivals for seventy-two days...plastering their heads with mud and wrapping strips of linen cloth below their breasts, women as well as men went about in groups of two or three hundred, and twice each day, reciting the dirge in a rhythmic chant, they sang the praises of the deceased, recalling his virtues."
Diodorus book 1, 72:1-2

Guests Brought Food to the Funeral

Guests brought food to the funeral, as we see in one of many scenes from the Papyrus of Ani below, restricting their own intake of food for 72 days.

Photo Credit: The Yorck Project

"... nor would they eat the flesh of any living thing or food prepared from wheat, and they abstained from wine and luxury of any sort."
Diodorus book 1, 72:2

Grieving Replaced All Other Acts of Life

"And no one would ever have seen fit to make use of baths or unguents or soft bedding, nay more, would not even have dared to indulge in sexual pleasures, but every Egyptian grieved and mourned during those seventy-two days as if it were his own beloved child that had died."
Diodorus book 1, 72:3

See the tears running down their faces.

Photo Credit: The Yorck Project

"The kingship... some assign this honour to the wealthiest, since they feel that these alone can come to the aid of the masses because they have the means ready at hand."
Diodorus book 3, 9:4

Quick Quiz:
What were the general mourning practices of ancient Egyptians?
What would ancient Egyptians do to their hair during the period of mourning?

The Body Ready for the Funeral

The opulence of the funeral and burial was based upon the deeds done while the deceased was alive.

Some Ethiopians "...*share a mortal nature and have come to receive immortal honours because of their virtue and the benefactions which they have bestowed upon all mankind*."
Diodorus book 3, 9:1

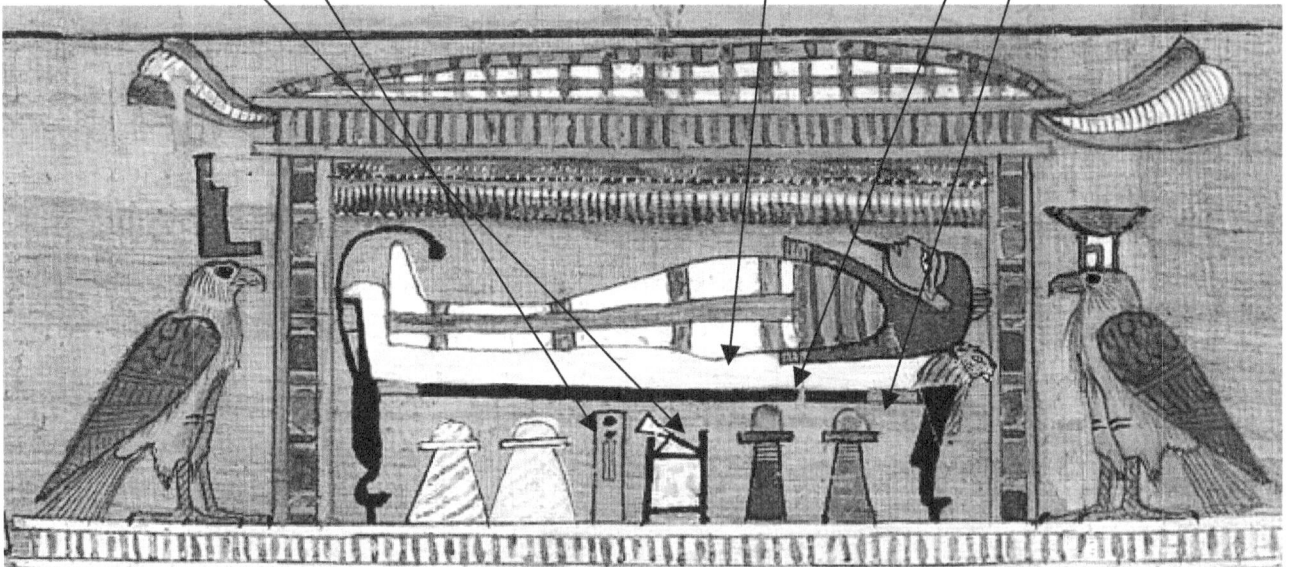

Photo Credit: *The Egyptian Book of the Dead: The Book of Going Forth by Day by James Wasserman et al*

Quick Quiz:
How do you think the Egyptians would have led their lives based on their burial customs?

Setting Up The Shrine

Below we see, kneeling on the left, a visitor to a shrine with three statues of a Ras and his two wives. Notice that the head of the statue is smaller than the head of the visitor, nearly half the size.

Photo Credit: The Egyptian Book of the Dead: The Book of Going Forth by Day by James Wasserman et al.

Transporting the Body

Photo Credit: The Egyptian Book of the Dead: The Book of Going Forth by Day by James Wasserman et al.

See the tear streaming down her face as she cries.

Photo Credit: The Egyptian Book of the Dead: The Book of Going Forth by Day by James Wasserman et al.

Quick Quiz:
Can you describe how a eulogy would be conducted in the ancient Egypt?
What does Diodorus tell us about burials about kings who were not good?

The Eulogy

Below are some other aspects of the ancient Egyptian eulogy, as written about by Diodorus.

Personal Remarks by Citizens Could Be Made During the Eulogy

"And when permission had been given to anyone who so wished to lay complaint against him..."

Priests Praised the Noble Deeds

"... the priests praised all his noble deeds one after another..."

The Citizens Gathered at and Attended the Funeral and Eulogy

"... the common people who had gathered in myriads to the funeral, listening to them, shouted their approval if the king had led a worthy life..."

Citizens Could Protest a King's Burial

"... but if he had not, they raised a clamour of protest. And in fact many kings have been deprived of the public burial customarily accorded them because of the opposition of the people; the result was, consequently, that the successive kings practised justice, not merely for the reasons just mentioned, but also because of their fear of the despite which would be shown their body after death and of eternal obloquy."

Diodorus book 1, 72:5-6

We will learn about how ancient Egyptian heroes were celebrated in book three!

Made in the USA
Las Vegas, NV
03 February 2025